Inspiring Stories for Girls

Girl, You're Amazing - A Collection
of Stories About Self-Confidence,
Courage, and Determination

Ruby Hart

Contents

The Courageous Princess: A Story of Bravery and Overcoming Fear

Princess Rosalie was one of the bravest girls in the kingdom.

From the day she was born, she was always up for a challenge and never backed down. When visitors came to the castle, and she was introduced to them, her mother and father, the king and queen, always used to tell the same story. The story about how, when she was only a few months old, she crawled out of her crib and tried to fight a goblin that had found its way onto the castle's first floor with nothing more than the toy sword she had from her Dragon Princess set.

Growing up, Rosalie was the bravest girl in town. She would always go on adventures with her friends, exploring the forests and mountains of her kingdom, even when the other kids were too scared.

She and her best friends would always run in the woods around the kingdom, climb the tallest trees, and fight off the little goblins in the forests. They would always return to the kingdom and tell the stories of their adventures to the other children at the round tables.

Rosalie thought she was unstoppable.

One very sunny day, Rosalie and her friends, Lily and Jack, decided to climb the tall mountain next to the kingdom. The three friends stood outside the main gate of the kingdom, ready for their adventure. Through the woods and forest land, the mountain stood up tall, rising up into the sky.

"Are you sure we want to go up?" asked Jack.

"Of course," said Rosalie, in her true, confident self. "You're not scared, are you, Jack?"

"No, it's just very high. I don't know if I'm scared of heights."

"You'll be fine, Jack," said Lily. "You've climbed many high trees and were never scared."

"Yes, but…"

"We'll be right with you, Jack," said Rosalie, smiling happily to show him that he was with good friends. He gave the group a nod and they pulled their bags onto their shoulders, setting off into the wild.

The forest was a place the children were used to. Rosalie had spent many weekends here since she was young, so they danced and skipped in the sun.

After many hours, the group found themselves at the foot of the mountain. Many adventurers came here to scout the area around the kingdom. The kids could see the tracks of horses and knights in the dried mud.

From the base, the mountain looked huge, rising up high into the sky, higher than the clouds. A small, rocky path led up the mountainside, heading out of view.

"Are we going all the way to the top?" said Jack, looking up to the top.

"We can go as far as we want!" said Rosalie.

They smiled and started a game of tag as they set off up the path. The friends played for a few more hours. They picked flowers and said hello to insects and bugs. They played tag, I-Spy, and many other games to pass the time. All while loving the beautiful views and the kingdom far away over the trees.

They stopped on a small stony ledge for lunch to catch their breath. Jack packed a picnic with all their favorite foods, like chocolate cake and sandwiches.

However, the peaceful lunch lasted only a short time. Just as Rosaline and Jack were putting out the picnic blanket, there was an incredible BOOM above them. It was the loudest BOOM Rosalie had ever heard, and the friends heard the sound echo across the mountain valley.

In an instant, black clouds rolled in, and the sky became gray and stormy. It felt like rain was going to fall.

As quickly as they could, the three jumped under the picnic blanket to hide.

"What was that?" Rosalie whispered. "What's happening? It wasn't supposed to rain today."

"I'm not sure," Jack replied. "But whatever it is, it sounds big and scary."

"It's just thunder, I think," said Lily. "I hope."

There was another huge BOOM, one that echoed across the valley.

Rosalie knew she was scared, but she also knew that if they stayed under the blanket, they would never find out what made that sound. She had to be brave and find out what was causing it, so she slowly stood up from under the blanket and stepped out into the open.

The thunder was still echoing across the valley, but it sounded farther away this time. Rosalie peered up into the sky and saw a magnificent sight.

It was a dragon!

Rosalie saw it for only a second as it flew behind one of the grumbling storm clouds. But she was still able to see how amazing it looked.

Dragons were not real! Dragons were supposed to be legends from the history books Rosalie read about in school. Monsters and scary animals that don't live today. Like dinosaurs!

But there it was. Flying high above her. She had seen it! A real-life dragon!

The dragon's scales were shining like gold, and its wings stretched out so far they were nearly as tall as the mountain. Rosalie felt a wave of feelings flow over her and she wanted to shout WOW at the top of her voice.

But she couldn't move.

Rosalie wanted to move to look at Jack and Lily, to see if they had seen the dragon too.

But she couldn't move.

Rosalie realized she was shaking as the cloud opened and rain poured. She was still looking up at the sky as the raindrops touched her face and rolled down her cheek.

"Rosalie," said Jack next to her. "Are you okay?"

"Dra... Dra... Dragon. In. The. Sky," she said, pointing up.

Lily and Jack's eyes widened as they looked up and saw the dragon too.

"Oh no! What is that? It is so BIG!" said Jack

"What if it sees us here? Do dragons eat explorers?" squealed Lily

The friends huddled together under the picnic blanket and pulled it over their heads, keeping them dry from the rain. They made a little hole and peered out to the sky, trying to see where the dragon was.

But the dragon was gone.

Suddenly, there was another loud BOOM as lightning erupted again, making the friends squeal and hold each other closer together. There was another roar, and the dragon was back.

Only this time...

IT WAS FLYING RIGHT TOWARDS THEM!

"RUN," shouted Jack.

The friends quickly grabbed the picnic blanket and ran away from the dragon as fast as they could. However, being on the small ledge, there was nowhere else to go without trying to climb down.

But the rocks were so wet, and the rain was so strong it would be IMPOSSIBLE to climb down!

"We have to find somewhere to hide quickly," said Rosaline. "The dragon is coming here! It's going to eat us!"

"Look, a cave. We can hide in here!" shouted Jack, pointing to a small opening in the mountain.

The three of them soon scrambled into the cave, pushing themselves further and further back into the darkness until there was no more room.

The cave went on for ages, and the light slowly disappeared until the three of them were in complete darkness. There was no sound for a few minutes until they heard the dragon roar again, and the ground shook from side to side.

"Oh no," said Lily. "I think the dragon landed in the cave as well!"

The three friends held on to each other tightly, not knowing what to do.

There was no way to contact the kingdom and get help! They would have to stay here.

After a few minutes, they heard the dragon slowly moving around in the darkness, searching for them. Rosalie's heart was pounding so hard she thought it would jump out of her chest.

"What are we going to do?" said Jack, trying to keep his voice from trembling.

"I think if we stay still," said Lily, "maybe the dragon will not see us, and it will leave?"

The three of them stayed silent for a while. The only sound came from the rain outside and the dragon's heavy breath right in front of them.

Rosalie was scared. Standing in the darkness, wet from the rain, with the biggest dragon ever in front of them, she had never been more scared in her whole life.

She did not know what to do. She knew that she did not want to be eaten by the dragon, that was for sure!

Standing there, she felt her friends get a little closer to her, and she suddenly felt another feeling. It was a strong feeling, stronger than feeling scared or worried about what would happen.

It was courage.

She thought about how brave her parents were and how they would never have let this dragon get away with eating their daughter. She thought about all the stories they had told her and how brave she could be if she believed in herself.

Rosalie felt her friends next to her, and with them being there, holding her hand, she knew she could do anything. She knew what she had to do.

If they stayed in the cave, they would be scared forever. And what if the dragon never leaves? Some of the books she had read said that some dragons sleep for a thousand years!

She knew what she had to do.

Taking a deep breath, she stepped forward, her friends still holding onto her.

With all the courage she had in her body, she shouted as loud as she could: "Leave us alone! We do not want to be eaten!"

There was a low rumbling.

The dragon did not move.

Rosalie felt her friends squeeze her hands tighter, and she took one more step forward.

"I said, LEAVE US ALONE!" she said, her voice echoing off the cave walls.

The dragon looked up and stared into the darkness. All Rosalie could see was the dragon's giant golden eyes looking in their direction. The dragon sniffed and breathed heavily, a little burst of smoke coming out of its nose.

Rosalie took a deep breath and slowly stepped forward once again, holding onto Lily and Jack's hands.

"Now, don't make me say it again," said Rosalie. "You best be getting out of here before I say something you don't want to hear."

"NOOOOOOOO!"

The dragon cried out so loudly that it echoed all through the cave. So loud that Rosaline, Jack, and Lily had to cover their ears to stop them from hurting!

"NOOOOOOOO!" The dragon roared again. "Don't make me go outside. It's cold and wet, and there is a storm outside!"

The three friends looked at each other, not knowing what to do.

Jack and Lily were still hiding behind Rosaline, scared of what would happen next. Rosaline, filled with the courage from her friends and her own strong heart, squeezed their hands, let them go, and stepped forward to the dragon, so close that the darkness no longer hid her.

"AHHH!" The dragon roared. "A LITTLE HUMAN."

The dragon moved so fast, moving its golden wing to hide its face. Although it was still big, the dragon tried its best to hide like a little ball.

Lightning struck once more outside the cave, and the dragon started to shiver even more!

Rosaline looked at the dragon and realized something. This dragon wasn't a scary dragon at all.

It was a SCAREDY dragon!

"It's okay," said Rosalie softly. "We won't hurt you; we just want to get out of the cave and go home."

Rosaline reached out and put her soft hand on the dragon's wing. Jack and Lily squealed and held each other closer together.

"I'm sorry that I shouted at you, Mr. Dragon. I was scared, but I now know that you were just as scared as I am."

The dragon looked up and slowly uncurled itself. Its golden eyes looked like two stars in the darkness.

"I... I... I am scared. I have never seen a thunderstorm before, and it is so loud and scary, and I wanted to hide in here."

Rosalie smiled and took another step closer to the dragon. "Come on, let us help you get out of the cave and show you how to get back home. And look, there is nothing to be scared of here. The thunderstorm won't hurt you. It is only a bit of rain!"

The dragon looked at Rosaline and her friends and could see the courage in their eyes. Slowly, it started to get up and followed them out of the cave.

They stepped outside and stepped into the thunderstorm. The rain was pouring down, but Rosalie, Lily, and Jack didn't care. They were laughing, dancing, and singing in the rain, and showing their new friend how to do it too!

After a few minutes, the dragon saw that there was indeed nothing to be scared of and joined the friends dancing in the rain!

And what a silly sight; seeing Princess Rosaline and her friends dancing in the rain on the mountain with a dragon of all creatures!

They danced for so long that the rain stopped, and a beautiful blue sky appeared with the best and biggest sun they had seen in a long time.

"Thank you for showing me how to be brave and courageous, Princess Rosaline. You will surely be a great queen one day!"

The dragon gave them a little nod and took off into the sky, breathing a big breath of fire as he flew off into the distance.

The three friends laughed and waved goodbye to their new friend, feeling so proud of themselves for being so brave.

"Come on," said Rosaline, turning to Jack and Lily, "Let's go home now." And they did.

The three friends had learned a precious lesson that day. No matter how scared you might be, there is always something to be brave about. All you need is a little courage and to feel how brave you can be in your heart!

Lucy Learns the Importance of Balance

Lucy was an intelligent girl and always did well in school.

In fact, you could say that Lucy loved school.

Seemingly every day, Lucy would come home with an armful of awards, certificates, and trophies. She was a star student! The teachers loved her, and her parents would always tell her and everyone they could just how proud they were of her and everything she did.

She loved it. The tests were straightforward. She always got the best grades. The competitions were always so much fun because she always got to win! She knew that she would go to college and university when she grew up. She'd be the best student and get the most amazing job.

Lucy's life was set up and it would be amazing.

However, one morning, Lucy woke up feeling a little different. Something just didn't feel right. It was a beautiful sunny day, right in the middle of summer. There was no rain. No mess in her bedroom. She had had no bad dreams the night before.

Usually, she would jump out of bed, rip open her curtains to say good morning to the sun, whistle back to the birds that usually sat on the tree outside her window, and get ready for another fantastic day at school.

But today was different. Lucy didn't feel motivated or enthusiastic. She felt like she was stuck in the mud and didn't want to move. Why would she work hard? she asked herself. What was the point? She felt as though it was not worth it anymore.

What was this feeling? She had never had it before.

She felt like she didn't want to go to school. She felt lost. Why should she go to school? What was the point of it all? To go to school and learn the lessons and do the tests. Get the grades and blah blah blah. Lucy didn't feel up for it anymore. But why?

Lucy couldn't even think. She didn't want to think. She just wanted to get back into bed and sleep the day away.

Still, with a heavy heart, Lucy got dressed and headed to school.

Her first class was tough. It was History, and the teacher was talking and writing notes as they always did, but everything felt like a blur. Lucy couldn't focus. She started to feel overwhelmed, and it almost felt like she was going to faint right there in the middle of the classroom.

"Lucy," asked the teacher after she put her head down on the table, "is everything alright?"

"Yes, just listening," she replied.

"Okay, well, pay attention!"

The teacher continued with the lesson, but Lucy couldn't pay attention. Her mind kept going to other thoughts, but she couldn't really tell what these thoughts were.

She drank some water and took some deep breaths, which helped to keep her awake, but she knew that something had changed for her.

Every lesson that day was the same.

Even during break time, Lucy would usually play with her friends on the playground and share any sweets they'd brought from home. This lunchtime, however, she just sat and watched her friends, feeling like an outsider.

When Lucy got home, she went straight up to her bedroom and cried in her bed.

"Why?" she asked herself. "Why was this happening to her?" Just a week ago, she was looking forward to school, and now she felt like it was an unbearable burden.

The next day, Lucy's alarm rang and she opened her eyes, hoping that she would feel like her usual self.

But she wasn't.

Lucy felt the same way she did the day before. She went to school, and the lessons went by in a blur. She sat on her own at lunchtime; and even when her friends asked her if she wanted to come and play her favorite game, Lucy said she just didn't feel like it.

In fact, every day that week felt the same, and it made Lucy feel so sad. Even her parents noticed and tried to make her feel better. They tried to talk to her, made her favorite tea, and let her stay up late to watch her favorite show, but none of it made her feel any better.

All she could do was sit and read her school books over and over again. She wanted to be the best.

Friday was a different day.

Lucy didn't feel any different from how she had been feeling. She still felt low and had no energy. She went to school, sat in assembly, and everything was okay until she got to math.

It was test day.

The same way she felt in the first lesson, Lucy's heart started to race, and her palms began to sweat. She was so nervous about the test that she convinced herself that it would be the end of the world if she got less than an A.

Like, actually the end of her world. She could not possibly fail, or she could not be the future superstar she was meant to be.

Lucy's teacher saw her expression as she walked up to the desk to take the test and asked if she was okay. Lucy shook her head and started to cry.

It was then that the teacher explained to her that it is okay to make mistakes and not everything she does needs to be perfect. She said that sometimes it is worth taking a step back to appreciate her achievements and find balance in her life.

Lucy didn't want to hear it. She had to ace this test.

She took a seat at her desk and started the test.

She couldn't do it. Just like she had been in lessons all week, the words in front of Lucy began to blur, and she couldn't read the paper. She tried for ten minutes before she started to cry. She didn't want her friends to see her, so she burst out of the room and ran away from the classroom as fast as possible.

"I don't want to do that test anymore. I don't want the grades, and I don't want the answer," she said to herself in her head again and again.

She ran and ran down the corridor and soon found herself at the door of the school garden. She opened the door quickly and slipped through.

She found a peaceful corner and sat down on the grass. She took a few deep breaths and closed her eyes.

When she opened them again, she saw her teacher, Miss Taylor, quietly coming into the garden. She took a seat next to Lucy and put her arm around her.

"Hey, Lucy," she said. "How are you?"

Lucy couldn't help but cry. She told Miss Taylor everything that had been running through her head and how scared she was that she would let everyone down if she didn't get an A on the test. She explained how her superstar future would be ruined, and all of her hard work would be for nothing.

Miss Taylor smiled at her.

"It's okay to make mistakes, Lucy. Not everything you do needs to be perfect," she said. "You don't have to ace everything, which is especially important because being perfect at everything is not the most important thing in the world. What is the most important thing in the world to you, Lucy?"

"I want to be happy," Lucy said.

Miss Taylor nodded and said, "You can still do great things with school while also taking care of yourself. Make sure to find a balance; if you ever feel overwhelmed, that's okay too. You can take a step back and appreciate what you have already achieved."

Lucy said nothing.

"It's amazing that you want to work hard and achieve so much with your life. It's so beautiful to see you so full of passion, and you're clearly very clever. I'm sure you are told that all the time. And it's important. But you can be happy right now. You are not living your life in the future. You are living your life right now!"

Lucy smiled, feeling a little better. She knew that there was no need to put so much pressure on herself and that it was okay to take a break when she needed one.

"What's your favorite flower in this beautiful garden, Lucy?" Miss Taylor asked.

Lucy pointed to a dahlia.

Miss Taylor crouched next to the flower and gave it a smell. She then beckoned Lucy to come next to her to smell it as well. It was gorgeous.

"Does smelling this beautiful flower make you feel happy?"

"It does," said Lucy.

"Well, that's how easy it is to be happy. If you work all the time, you will be unable to smell the flowers and take a break. You won't find balance, and that's why it is so important."

"It's okay to take a step back, appreciate what you have already achieved, and find balance in your life."

Lucy took a deep breath and smiled. She thanked Miss Taylor for the talk and gave her a big hug.

She knew she could care for herself and still do great things with school. She was determined never to forget Miss Taylor's lesson in the school garden that day. She was always determined to find balance in whatever she was doing in life and take care of herself.

The Spell of Being Everything

The Spell of Being Everything was a spell that many young girls wished they could cast.

It's a spell as old as time found throughout the ages of history. The spell is simple.

Simply wave the magic wand and the caster can become whoever or whatever they want to be. People use it for good, like pretending to be trolls to scare away other trolls, or disguising themselves as a mother bird to protect a little baby bird until the mother gets home.

It can also be used to help people go on amazing adventures and make everyone happy along the way.

The Spell of Being Everything is a very powerful spell, but for hundreds of years, it was a forgotten spell. So old that it became a rumor, then a myth, then a legend. Finally, it was forgotten about forever.

That was, until, it was discovered by the most unlikely young girl, Ruby.

Ruby was a normal girl, just like you or me. She was in school, had friends, and lived at home with her parents. But something was missing.

One day while walking through a forest near her house, she stumbled upon an old tree with a glowing wand on the ground in front of it.

Strange, Ruby thought to herself. She was getting a bit old to believe in gnomes and fairies, but this clearly looked like a fairy wand that may have been lost. When she picked it up, it felt real, like it had some magic in it. It made her fingertips feel like popping candy, and she felt lighter than she had before.

Ruby twirled it in her fingers, lovingly looking at the wand's very faint, but still beautiful, magical glow.

"Hello," Ruby called out into the woods. "Is anyone here?"

No one answered.

"Hello? I think someone has lost their wand," Ruby said, but nobody responded. The forest was silent.

She looked around the tree and at the base of it found a small red box. Even though it had a keyhole on the front, it wasn't locked.

Inside was a scroll that said, "The Spell of Being Everything. Be careful."

"The spell of Being Everything?" she whispered to herself. She had never heard of such magic.

"Well," she thought to herself, "I can't possibly leave this magic just lying around here for anyone to just find and use. I best take it home and look after it."

She decided to take a piece of paper and a pen out of her school rucksack and write a little note saying that she had the magic wand, and she was happy to give it back to whoever came to claim it. She was just keeping it safe. She hid the note in the roots of the tree and skipped off home.

She forgot about the wand for the rest of the night. She only once checked it was safe in the bottom drawer of her bedside table before going to sleep.

However, that night, Ruby had the craziest, most vivid dream she'd had in a long time.

In it, the magic wand transformed itself into people she knew. In a swish of light and magic, it became her parents, her friends, and even herself.

"What is this?" she asked in the dream, scared but also intrigued.

Suddenly a voice appeared from nowhere, "You have stumbled upon one of the oldest magical spells known to humankind: The Spell of Being Everything."

The voice explained how it was possible to make yourself look like anyone or anything you wanted, just by using the wand.

When Ruby awoke that morning, she remembered the dream and instantly knew what to do with her newfound magical gift. She grabbed her new wand and ran out of her bedroom door. She decided to use it to try and make everyone around her happy.

She went downstairs and sat at the table while her mother and father were having breakfast.

"Hmm," said her father as he read the newspaper. "The news looks bad again."

"I know," said her mother.

"I can't believe it's still happening."

"What was it they said on the TV?"

"I don't know who to believe anymore."

Ruby didn't know who or what her parents were talking about, but it was clear the mood was sad. It was like this every morning. And every night. All they did was complain about the world and the people in it. She couldn't actually remember the last time they were happy.

Underneath the table, the wand started to glow warmly. Ruby could feel its warmth against her leg, and she stopped eating her breakfast for a moment. Maybe I can make this better, she said to herself.

She remembered how the note said to be careful, but then again, maybe the note was old. Perhaps this wand really was magic, and if it was, then she could do amazing things with it. She could make the world a better place. After all, isn't that what magic should be used for?

Ruby slipped the wand out of her book bag and gave it a few squishes under the table, wishing that she'd still be herself, only as funny as a world-class comedian.

The wand squished and there was a little flash under the table, but her parents were tool wrapped up in the newspapers to notice.

Ruby sat for a minute or two. Her body didn't feel different. She didn't think any different. It didn't seem like anything had changed. Well, might as well try it, she thought to herself.

"Oh, and now the government is trying this. Again. Can you believe it?" her dad said without lowering the paper.

"Hey dad," Ruby chirped up. "Can I tell you a joke?"

"Of course, darling," he said, still not looking away from the paper.

Ruby didn't say anything for a second. She didn't really know any jokes, but suddenly, a whole storm of them came into her mind. She went with the first one she settled on.

"Why did the scarecrow win a prize?"

"Why?"

"Because he was outstanding in his field!"

Ruby's dad suddenly burst into laughter.

"Oh my, Ruby. That's actually really funny. Where did you hear this joke?"

"Just around," Ruby said, smiling to herself.

"Tell us another one!" said her mother.

"Okay. What do sprinters eat before running a race? Nothing. They fast."

Both Ruby's mom and dad burst into even more laughter. They quickly put away their newspaper and asked for more. And more. And more. All breakfast, Ruby told her parents one joke after another, making them laugh even harder each time.

"These are so great," said her father. "Where did you hear them?"

"Oh, I just made them up!" Ruby replied, with a wink. "Here's another one! What did the fish say when it hit the wall? Dam!"

Her parents couldn't help but laugh at her funny jokes, and their moods had well and truly lifted.

"Oh, well, I'm late for work, but that doesn't matter," said her father, who was close to tears and barely able to stand up.

"I'll give you a lift," said Ruby's mother. "Can you get the bus, Ruby?"

"Of course! I'll see you tonight!"

On the bus, Ruby thought about her new found power. The wand was really powerful stuff, but she was going to have to be careful to make sure she used it properly. But Ruby was happy. She had made her parents happy and maybe this happiness would last for a long time! She would have to wait and see. In the meantime, she was curious to see what else she could do with this newfound power.

When she got to school, she sat through the register, through the first assembly, and then her first class began.

Urgh. Math was always so hard.

As always, the teacher was going on about sums and divisions. Ruby tried her hardest to keep up. She looked at her textbook but couldn't figure out what the teacher was talking about or what was going on.

She was about to give up hope and go back to daydreaming like she usually did. However, a thought popped into her head. She remembered the wand in her pocket and had an idea. With a few discrete swishes, she turned herself into a math genius!

In an instant, the wand glowed warmly, and Ruby suddenly found herself understanding the equations!

In no more than a few seconds, Ruby was enjoying math more than ever before. She read several pages of the textbook and understood everything that was written perfectly. She turned page after page, and there was not a drop of confusion in her mind.

"Ruby," said her teacher. "Are you paying attention?"

"Yes, of course," Ruby replied, closing the textbook.

"Okay, well would you like to tell me the answer to the question I just asked?"

Ruby hadn't been paying attention. She had been too absorbed by her textbook. She looked to the board to see the equation that had been written out. It made perfect sense.

"The answer is 62. You just have to remember to divide the 32 first."

"Well, very well-done Ruby. That's most excellent," the teacher said, nodding. He was clearly impressed, especially since Ruby didn't usually answer questions. In fact, she couldn't remember answering a single question since starting this class!

Her classmates knew this, and looked at her in shock. As worksheets were given out to the class, the classmates around Ruby started to ask her question after question. She knew all the answers, and was more than happy to help!

As Ruby was helping herself and her classmates with all the questions, the teacher came over.

"Ruby," said the teacher. "I am so proud of you! You must have been working so hard and it shows. Keep up the great work!"

Ruby beamed with pride and put her wand away in her pocket, feeling content and full of joy.

At lunch, Ruby and her friends sat on the playground.

"I'm bored," said one of her friends.

"There's no games we haven't already played," another said.

"I wish we had a massive climbing frame with a slide and nets."

"Well," said Ruby cunningly. "I may be able to help!"

Ruby turned her back to her friends, swished her wand under her coat, and in an instant, she had magically transformed herself into a giant climbing frame! Her friends were in awe.

"This is the best day ever," all her friends cheered.

"You are so cool," said one of them.

They spent the whole lunchtime playing, running up and down the nets and sliding down the slide. It was a great way to get their minds off of their worries and just have fun. The rest of the day was simply amazing.

At the end of the day, Ruby was exhausted, but she also felt a great sense of accomplishment. She had used her wand to make everyone around her happy and in turn that made her feel joyous too. "This is what magic should be used for," she thought to herself.

That night when she went to bed, Ruby put away her wand. She had had the best day and couldn't wait to see what tomorrow bought.

The next day, Ruby jumped out of bed, full of energy, ready to use the wand for all kinds of magical adventures.

She ran downstairs, transforming into a comedian again, and said good morning to her parents.

"Good morning, Ruby," they said in unison. Dad poked his cereal with his spoon and Mom looked sadly at her phone.

"Hey mom. Hey Dad. Is everything okay?"

"Yes and no sweetie," her dad said. "I was very late for work yesterday and I couldn't stop laughing all day. I laughed so much, even when my boss was telling me off, and he got very angry and asked me to not come in today."

Ruby gulped.

"Oh dad, I'm so sorry. Is there anything I can do?"

Dad shook his head and smiled.

"No sweetie," he said. "I just need to accept that sometimes things don't go the way we expect them to."

Ruby hugged him tightly and accepted his words. If she hadn't been so funny, Dad would have been able to go to work and wouldn't have gotten in trouble.

Ruby went off to school saddened, but vowed to make it up to her dad when she got home with her newfound magic powers.

When she arrived at school, Ruby noticed that everyone was talking about a girl in the class who apparently could do all sorts of amazing things with her magical wand. While waiting for the first bell, everyone kept coming up to her and asking her to do all these crazy things.

"Turn into a plane and take me to a sunny place!"

"Turn into a pizza bar!"

"Come on Ruby, turn into a cinema so we can watch movies all day!"

But Ruby didn't want to turn into anything. She just wanted to hang out with her friends, but all they wanted her to do was to turn into someone or something else. In the end, she hid in the bathroom until the first bell rang. It was Math again.

"Hello everyone," the teacher said. "Since everyone was doing so amazingly yesterday with their math work, I decided to move the end of the term test to today so we can get it out the way and start working on next year's work. I'm so proud of you all, and from what I saw yesterday, you should all do well."

"Oh no," the class groaned. "Not a test."

Ruby and her classmates knew that it was only because of the wand that everyone knew all the answers, and now it was backfiring. Everyone turned to Ruby as the teacher handed out the tests.

"Are you going to help us with the answers Ruby?"

"Excuse me class, no talking while the test is underway."

Everyone scowled at Ruby. The test was very difficult and went on for a long time. At the end, Ruby was relieved and knew she had done her best, although it was nowhere near what the class was doing yesterday.

"Thanks a bunch Ruby," said one classmate on the way out. "I definitely failed the test."

"Yeah, thanks a lot Ruby, I thought you were supposed to be cool!" said another.

Ruby walked out of the class feeling very down. Everyone was mad at her and she realized that although her wand could be handy when it came to playing, it couldn't do anything when it came to real-life situations.

What could she do? Transform into someone who could make it all better? Maybe, but she didn't want to. Nobody was talking to her and it's not like she wanted or could trick people into liking her.

At lunch, everyone was still in a bad mood. Ruby thought about turning herself into a large climbing frame again, with nets and swings and slides. Instead, she decided to turn herself into a clown, but nobody paid any attention. Everyone was too sad.

On the way home from school, Ruby thought about everything that had happened over the last few days. She had tried to make everyone happy using the Spell of Being Everything, and while it was fun, the fun never lasted.

"What did I do wrong? How could I do things better?" she thought to herself.

When she got home, she sat on her bed and thought about it. A few minutes passed and she heard a light knocking at the bedroom window. Looking over, she saw a small fairy fluttering around, sparkling in the sunlight.

"Hello Ruby," the fairy said. "I'm here to give you a very special gift with a very special message. It's a thank you for looking after my magic."

"Your magic?" Ruby said.

"Yes," the fairy said. "The wand is too powerful for children and it

was my job to make sure that it didn't get misused. As I am sure you're finding out."

"Yes, I am. I tried to use it for good and to make everyone around me happy, but I ended up making them sadder. How do you do it?"

"That is what happens. And that's for a very simple reason."

Ruby leaned in, eager to hear what the fairy had to say.

"The world loves you for who you are, not what you pretend to be," the fairy said in a calming voice. "You don't need to be anything other than you, because that's what makes you so special. That's why you have so many friends and people who love you. So never forget that."

The fairy flew away, leaving Ruby with a smile on her face and a new way of looking at the world. From that day forward, Ruby decided to be herself and not try to be someone else. She learned that it was better to be herself, and the world loved her for it.

The wand was put away forever and Ruby learned to accept herself. She was a gift and the world loved her for it.

Whenever she felt down, she would remember what the fairy told her and be reminded to be herself and love who she was.

And she vowed to always remind others to do the same.

Emily and the Fox

Emily loved her life. She went to a nice school and had some really beautiful friends. She was confident, had lots of sleepovers, was doing well in her classes, and basically just loved how she spent her days. She was a happy girl, and she knew it.

That was until her dad got a new job, which meant that after the summer holidays, Emily had to start a new school. When Emily heard the news, she cried for what felt like forever.

She couldn't stop herself as she just felt so sad. She knew what it meant. She had seen the same thing happen to some of the girls and boys she saw on TV shows. She would no longer live in the house she grew up in and had to say goodbye to all her friends.

Of course, they said they would all stay in touch and call her all the time, but Emily knew it wouldn't be the same. People drift apart when they don't see each other often, and they'll probably just forget about her.

The week of the move, Emily did nothing but sit quietly in her room, looking at all her things packed into cardboard boxes. Emily's parents came in to see if she was okay.

"Hey Emily, how are you getting on?"

Emily didn't say anything. She just sat on her bed with her knees pulled into her chest and tried not to think about anything at all. Her dad came and sat next to her, and gave her a little cuddle.

"You're going to be fine, you know. I moved away from my hometown when I was younger and felt the same. But give it a few weeks, and you'll be making new friends in no time. You're a bright, happy, and cheerful young girl. You'll have no problems. I'll make sure of it. Mom and I are here for you through it all!"

"Think of it as a new adventure full of fun," said Emily's mom, sitting on the other side of her. "Who knows what exciting and interesting people you could meet?"

Emily nodded, and her parents left to carry on packing. She thought about looking at it that way. An adventure. A chance to go to new lands and meet new people. That was quite an exciting way to look at it, Emily thought. All the princesses and explorers in her books and in the movies had to go away to far-off places at some point and meet new people, and they ended up okay. Maybe she could be like that.

And so Emily was excited for the move.

She was looking forward to meeting new people and discovering a new school. She was so excited, until the first day of school. She woke up with a very strange feeling she had not felt in a long time. A feeling like when you go on stage to perform in the school show, and you know that everybody, all the kids and all the parents, are watching.

Emily's dad dropped her off at the front gate, and Emily found herself feeling nothing but shy.

"Oh no," Emily thought to herself. "How will I make friends and discover new places if I can't talk to anyone?" She looked around at all the kids. They all had their friend groups and knew each other. The boys were playing football in the playground. All the girls were chatting and laughing in little groups. What could she even say to these kids? What if they really didn't like her and said she was weird because she came from a different school?

She wanted so much to make friends, but fear held her back.

She tried to make friends with the girl sitting next to her in the first class. She seemed lovely. Her name was Anna, and she had beautiful red hair that flowed down her back. Emily wanted to say something nice about her hair and thought it would be a really great way to start making a friend. However, when she tried to talk, nothing came out of her mouth, and she was so embarrassed. She felt like everyone was judging her, so she began to back away from potential conversations.

What are they thinking? she thought to herself. Were they thinking she was weird, or maybe not cool enough?

Emily soon found herself in a bit of a pickle. What would she do if she couldn't find any friends and nobody liked her? She couldn't take this for years.

At lunchtime, she tried to talk to a few other girls playing hopscotch near the school field, but she couldn't bring herself to do it. Instead, she just sat on one of the benches on her own and tried to make it look like she wasn't staring in their direction.

A few girls seemed to like the same clothes as her. Before going up to them, she tried to think of something to say, but nothing came out.

It felt like everyone who was walking past was staring at her,

making her feel even more self-conscious.

The rest of the day went by the same, and before long, it was time to go home. Her mom picked her up.

"How was school today, sweetie? Did you meet lots of new people?"

"No. Not a single one. I'm too shy. I couldn't even say anything to anyone."

"Well, you just need to give it more than one day. I'm sure today you were busy looking around the new school and figuring out where you were going. Very busy. I'm sure tomorrow will be better."

"Yeah," said her dad. "Maybe just start with trying to talk with one person and go from there! You have nothing to be ashamed of, sweetie. You're a lovely girl; anybody would be lucky to have you as their friend."

Emily smiled a little but didn't believe them. It was never going to work, and she would be lonely forever.

"Can I go for a walk? I just want to be by myself for a bit," Emily asked when they got home. Her parents nodded and told her to be back in time for dinner.

Emily left the house and started to wander around the new neighborhood. After a few minutes, she reached the edge of the street that sat next to a small bit of woodland. "Hmm," Emily thought to herself, "this is more like it. Quiet time in nature." She stepped off the street and into the trees.

She wandered around the quiet woods for a bit, thinking about life and missing her hometown. She missed her friends and wondered what they were up to right now. Were they thinking of her? Were they missing her as much as she missed them?

After a while, Emily came across a small, gorgeous lake with the sun beaming down. Emily decided to have a short break and enjoy the scene. She found a nice log to put her back against and sat down but instantly heard a horrible cry!

Emily stood up so quickly to see what had made the sound. There, laying out next to the log, was a fox.

The fox startled and ran off into the woods. However, it didn't disappear from view completely, and instead stopped by a nearby tree, circled around the truck, and looked straight back at Emily. The forest fell silent.

"I'm sorry Mr. or Miss Fox. I didn't mean to scare you," said Emily.

The fox said nothing, but continued to look at her with an almost-wise look in his or her eyes.

"I didn't mean to take you by surprise, that's all."

The fox kept looking, but said nothing. Instead it sat down on one of the roots of the tree and started to lick its paw, but never once taking its eye off Emily.

"Look at me," she said out loud, "talking to a fox in the middle of the woods. I must be going mad."

She sat in silence with the fox for a few minutes. It didn't seem scared or afraid, more curious and interested in what Emily was doing. She slowly sat herself down on the log, never taking her eye off the fox, in case it ran away.

Being able to see it properly now that she had calmed down and didn't feel so bad, she could see it had the most brilliant orange fur, gorgeous brown eyes, and the slenderest figure. Emily thought about all the beautiful foxes she had seen in her story books growing up, and this fox was far more beautiful than any of them.

And it was real!

"Can I ask you a question, fox?" she said. The fox said nothing, and continued to look straight at Emily.

Emily hesitated, knowing she wouldn't get a response, but secretly hoped she would. Besides, it was nice to actually talk out loud. Something she hadn't done all day.

"How come you're not running away? Are you a friendly fox? Normally wild animals run away from humans. They're usually too shy to sit and hang around."

Emily sat still and watched. The fox watched back. Emily decided to try and trick the beautiful animal into believing she had some food. She pulled up bits of twig, broke them up, and softly threw them towards the fox's feet. The fox lent down slightly and sniffed the ground, and sat back up, eyes locked on Emily's.

"Ah, sorry. I knew you were too smart for that. I do that with my neighbor's cat sometimes. Not saying that you're anything like a cat. Oh, I'm just being silly. I'm sorry Fox."

Emily started to cry. She had had such a bad day at school, felt so lonely, and missed all her friends back home. She just wanted someone to talk to. Now she was trying to trick a fox in the woods, even though he had been so nice to sit with her by the tree to keep her company.

Suddenly, something very strange happened.

The fox stood up and stretched its back legs. First the left one. Then the right one. Then it shook the debris off his fur, licked himself once and started to walk towards Emily! Emily couldn't believe it. She froze completely still, and didn't want to make any sudden movements, in case she scared it off.

The fox walked right to her, stopped and looked at her for a few seconds, and almost seemed to smile at her. Smile? At her? A human? Surely that wasn't possible. But here she was in the woods seeing it for herself. The fox then casually kept walking past her, up a small hill in which a tall tree was growing, looked back, nodded once, and then disappeared out of sight.

Emily didn't know what to make of the situation. As she walked back through the woods and back towards her house, she kept a keen eye open for the fox again, hoping to catch a glimpse of its beautiful orange fur and even warmer smile.

But, lo and behold, it was nowhere to be seen.

As Emily got into bed that night, she couldn't stop thinking about the fox.

Why had it not been scared to be around her?

Most animals were shy, but the fox just stood there, just looking at each other and feeling very peaceful.

And then it hit her.

Of course, why was the fox scared? What did it have to be shy of? Emily wasn't going to hurt him, and maybe the fox felt that. She was just a girl looking for a friend. And it was the same with school!

There was no one there that wanted to scare her or make her feel bad. They're all just boys and girls who want to have friends and have a good time in life. Emily laughed at herself in the darkness of her room.

What was there to be shy of? Why couldn't she be braver like the fox and just enjoy being around other people, and in the world? Well, she decided to do just that.

And she knew she wasn't going to squash anyone like she did the fox, and even he didn't seem to mind that, so what was there to worry about?

Emily thanked the fox and sent all the love she could for him out into the world, knowing that it would reach him somehow. From that day onwards, she felt more courageous. She was still shy at times, but she could now talk to people without feeling scared or embarrassed.

She made friends with some of her classmates and even joined a few after-school clubs.

Emily was no longer shy, and she now dared to speak up for herself. She felt proud of how far she had come and thankful that the fox helped her find her inner strength.

Thanks to him, Emily now knew that it was okay to be different and could overcome anything with self-confidence and courage.

Melissa and the Magic Backpack

Once upon a time, there was a girl named Melissa.

Melissa was a kind and sweet girl who absolutely loved life and everything in it. She loved people. She loved things. She loved spending time in nature and running around in the rain just as much as she loved watching movies and reading books in bed. However, above all else in this world, Melissa's absolute favorite thing in the whole wide world was collecting things.

She loved to collect things because they helped her to remember all the amazing things she saw and did. She had rocks from the walks she went on with her parents. She collected small jars of sand during her trips to the beach. She also had pine cones, twigs from autumn, and a little jar of rain from the April showers last year.

She also tried to collect coins, stamps, postcards, envelopes, brochures from zoos, wrappers from the chocolate biscuits she ate, and so many more. It was a lot of fun, and it was always a great afternoon when Melissa got to dive into her collections to remember all the beautiful things she'd done over the years.

But, Melissa had a problem.

Over the years, she had collected so many things that she was starting to run out of space. Her drawers were overflowing. Her wardrobe doors were bursting so much that they popped open multiple times a day. Even her pockets were overflowing.

And Christmas was just around the corner, and there were lots of things to collect! What was she going to do?

On one particular day, she returned home from the local Christmas fair and had collected a few leaflets, but this time, her room had really reached its limit.

She wanted to put the leaflet on her desk, but it was full of her collections. She tried the drawers, but these were overflowing with school clothes and her drawings. Melissa's shelves were full of books, and under her bed was filled with teddies, sticks, and old socks.

"Hmm," Melissa said to herself. "What can I do with all these things?"

Just then, something caught her eye. It was a tiny glimmer in the corner of her room. "What was that?" she thought to herself. She didn't remember putting anything that glimmered in that corner of the room next to her dolls and car collection. There may have been a lot of stuff in this room, but Melissa was organized and knew where everything was at all times.

She crawled closer and saw that it was a backpack! "Strange," she thought. She hadn't seen a backpack like this before, and had no idea how it got there. She looked closer and realized that it was not just an old backpack, but a magic backpack!

The bag was made from beautiful blue velvet, with golden embroidery on the edges and straps. The bag seemed to glimmer in the light, and Melissa was so excited! She quickly reached for it, and the moment she touched it, a voice spoke in her head: "This bag is magical. You can put an unlimited number of things inside, and it will never get full or heavy!"

Melissa was so excited at the idea of a magical backpack that she didn't even think about where the backpack had come from or who had put it in her room. She didn't even see the sneaky little goblin that had placed it there to play a trick on her for fun. The goblin watched her, a sneaky grin on its face and it knew about how much mischief this could cause. With one last look, not wanting to be seen by any humans, the goblin snapped its fingers and disappeared back to its magic realm.

Melissa was delighted, stuffing in her Christmas Fair leaflet and seeing it drop down to the bottom of the bag where she couldn't see it.

"But, how am I supposed to get the things out again," she asked no one in particular.

"Just think about what you want, stick your hand in, and it will come," said the voice in her head.

Melissa thought about her Christmas leaflet, put her hand carefully into the bag, and within a few seconds, she felt the paper between her fingers. She gripped tighter and pulled out the leaflet. She couldn't believe it. This really was a magic bag!

Melissa wanted to test things out even more. She grabbed random things from her room and dropped them into the bag. She opened the top and watched them fall into the white light of the bag and out of view.

"This is amazing," Melissa thought to herself. "I wonder what else I can fit into this bag."

For the next hour, Melissa ran around the house, putting everything she could into the bag. She put pens, pencils, and files from her dad's office. She put all the plates, cups, mugs, knives, and forks from the drawers and cupboards in the kitchen. She put all the food in the fridge, ran into the garden, and dropped in all the tools from the garden shed.

"Wow, this bag is amazing," Melissa thought to herself. She looked down at all the things she had collected and decided to take a break, summoning one of the snacks she had put in the bag. She looked down at the bag and noticed something strange.

It was bigger. Yes, that was it. The bag still weighed the same and felt as light as it was empty, but it was way bigger than it used to be. Even the hole at the top where Melissa put things into the bag was bigger. She had been so excited that she hadn't even noticed the bag was now almost as tall as her.

"I wonder how far this can go," she thought to herself and took the bag around to the front of the house. On the driveway, there was her parents' car. Mom and Dad had gone out for the day to see a friend, and Melissa was left to look after the house.

"I think the car would probably be safer if it was in the backpack where I could look after it properly," she thought to herself. With this in mind, she laid the backpack on the ground, opened up the top hole as wide as she could, and pulled it to the front of the car.

The car just about managed to slip inside, so Melissa ran around to the back and pushed the backpack all the way down over the car until it was gone completely. The bag grew a little bit bigger until the car was completely gone. And it still didn't weigh more than a piece of paper!

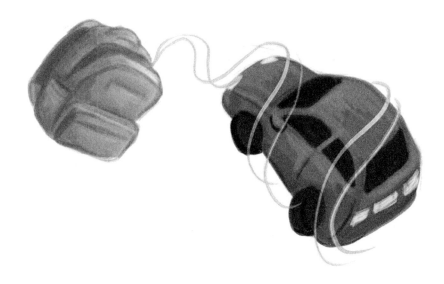

"This is amazing," thought Melissa. And then the idea struck her.

I CAN COLLECT EVERYTHING!

I can have all the toys in the world. All the snacks. All the food. All the movies. All for ME!

Thinking nothing of it, Melissa aimed the backpack down the street and started to push it. Since it was so light, it moved so easily, collecting everything in its path.

It ate cars, letterboxes, and hedgerows. After a few minutes of running up and down the street, the backpack was even big enough to start collecting houses. "This is amazing," thought Melissa. I will have so much stuff!"

For the next few hours, Melissa ended up in the city, collecting everything she could find, from people to skyscrapers. The bag was so big that it seemed to have a life of its own. It moved around the city, gobbling up everything while she sat on the very top and enjoyed the ride. It was amazing to see how easily the backpack collected everything.

Back on the ground, the people around her noticed what was happening, but they couldn't do anything about Melissa's greed. She just kept taking and taking. She was so high up on the backpack that she couldn't even hear them shouting at her to stop!

A few more hours passed, and most of the city was collected in the backpack, and Melissa sat on the top as high as the clouds!

"Wow," she thought to herself, "there's nothing down there on the ground anymore. I've collected everything in the whole world. I can't wait to tell my… friends and family," Melissa gulped.

She had been so excited about collecting everything she could and having all the toys and things she could possibly have that she hadn't stopped to think about how this would affect everyone else.

Suddenly, Melissa realized what she had done. She had taken away things that belonged to other people, and they were all so sad and disappointed in her. Tears streaming down her face, Melissa slowly started to understand the importance of sharing and giving.

She climbed up her bag and tried to push more things into it, but she slipped and fell in, disappearing with the items she had taken from others.

Inside the bag, Melissa was stuck in the dark. She was trapped between her collections, unable to move or breathe properly. She was scared and alone, trapped between cars and buildings and people crying out for help.

Melissa thought of her parents and wondered where they were. In an instant, her parents appeared right next to her!

"Mom! Dad!" she cried out, "I'm so sorry; I don't know why I did all this!"

"It's okay, lovely. It was a pretty bad thing to do, but what we need to focus on right now is making it better. Can we do that?"

"I know, and I'm sorry. I'll tell everyone I'm sorry. I don't know how to fix this, though."

"Well," said her Dad, looking around, "it seems to me that this bag is so full that it's going to pop, so maybe it's time to give it a little helping hand."

Melissa nodded and knew what she had to do. She felt around and started to make her way through the stuff in the backpack. Before long, she found herself at the edge of the backpack, feeling the soft velvet fabric at her fingertips. Her Dad was right. The velvet was so tight that it sure felt like it was going to pop any time now.

Melissa thought about everything she had collected. There must have been a pin or a sewing set in one of the many houses she collected. She thought long and hard about a pin.

In an instant, a small thumbtack appeared in her hand. Perfect.

Melissa reached out with all her strength and pushed the pin deep into the side of the backpack. There was an almighty BOOOOOOOM, and a bright light suddenly appeared, blinding everyone for miles around.

It took a few minutes for the sound to stop and for the bright light to fade, but when she opened her eyes, it seemed as though everything that was inside the bag was flying out in all directions!

Skyscrapers flew back across the sky to where they had been collected, as did cars, lamp posts, and even people! People landed back where they had been standing and breathed a big sigh of relief!

Melissa fell out of the bag, too, right where she had fallen in; her parents were next to her. They all felt exhausted but relieved to be back in the light.

The bag still whizzed around in the air like someone had let air out of a balloon. It whizzed around for a few minutes before flopping to the ground in front of Melissa, torn up and ripped in so many different places.

All around them, people were smiling and laughing, glad to be okay and that their belongings were returning back to them.

The people around her were astonished by the number of items that had come out of the bag and realized what Melissa had been doing. They helped her clean up the mess, and slowly but surely, Melissa started to share her items with everyone.

Since then, Melissa has learned her lesson and never forgets that it's always better to share than hoard. It's never okay to steal from people and to instead be grateful for what we have, instead of constantly needing more, more and MORE!!

Everyone Is Good at Something, Not Everything

Ella had never failed at anything in her whole life.

She was good at school, she was good at sports, and she was even good at magic. Everyone knew that Ella could cast a spell faster, more beautifully, and more amazingly than everyone else.

Once, she was able to cast a giant firework of a bird high in the sky above the school on her first try, and everyone was so impressed. Other girls wish they could be her; her parents and teachers couldn't be prouder.

However, being the smartest, best, and most wonderful girl in school didn't come without some downsides. Most importantly, Ella felt kind of alone in school. When Ella looked around her, she noticed that her friends weren't quite as great as she was.

They got bad grades, and some could never make the team in sports tryouts. Most of them weren't as good at magic as she was. Ella didn't understand why they couldn't be like her, and she started to feel a little bit superior.

She was still friends with them, and they were lovely people to be around. However, she couldn't help but feel as though she was a little bit better than them.

Sometimes this showed. When her friend Jessica did a little poorly on a test, Ella replied: "Hey, you just need to do it a little better, and you'll be okay."

When her friend Jack tried out for the football team, Ella said: "Don't worry; there are just people who are better than you. Maybe you can try again next year. Just remember to run faster."

Of course, things like this didn't help, and sometimes Ella upset people without realizing it. She could never understand it because all they needed to do was be better, and she was just reminding them of that.

But there was no denying that Ella was good. That's why Ella got invited to run in the Magic Sports Day race, representing humans against fairies, goblins, and all sorts of magical beings. She knew for sure that she would win; she had even been practicing extra hard for weeks in advance.

"I can't believe it," her friends squealed around her when they found out. "We're so excited. We're going to watch you on TV and everything!"

Ella was a little nervous, but she was excited. She had been the best in her school for years and had no doubt that she would do amazingly in the competition since she was doing her favorite thing: running.

Ella had loved running for years and was so good at it, winning multiple events against other schools time and time again. She had this, and she would make her parents, teachers, friends, and school proud.

She left for the competition and arrived on the big day. There were all kinds of magical creatures and beings here, from warlocks to wizards to unicorns to stunning dragons.

However, once she started to see the events, she started to panic, and Ella realized she didn't have a chance. All the magical beings were incredibly magical or had a natural advantage over her that she couldn't compete with.

The unicorns had more legs, the fairies had magic, and the dragons didn't even have to run - they could just fly instead! The goal of the race was to get across the line as quickly as possible, but the rules didn't say how or why!

Ella was furious. All her hard work was for nothing, and she was starting to feel a little bit jealous of the magical creatures.

"Hey," she said. "This isn't fair! Unicorns have more legs, fairies have magic, and dragons don't even have to run!"

"Well," replied the Games Master. "That may be true, but that's okay; I'm sure you'll win at something."

"But I'm not in any of the other competitions; I'm here to run!"

"Well, that's okay. Just do your best. That's what we're all here for! Just have some fun doing it, and don't forget to run fast!"

Ella didn't want to hear it. She stormed off and went back to the area that was for humans. As she walked, she heard the rude comments from the other magical beings.

"Ha," said the unicorn to their friends. "Did she really think she had a chance?"

Ella ran with tears forming in her eyes. She started to pass the fairies and heard them all giggling to themselves.

"Well, this is going to be anti–climactic," said one fairy.

Ella quickly wiped away her tears and stopped in front of the fairies.

"You know what," she said, "everyone is allowed to be good and bad at different things. We should be kind to each other. Maybe I can't get across the line fast, but I can do plenty of other amazing things!"

The fairies nodded in agreement and went back to laughing. Ella shrugged at them as the realization came to her. For the first time, Ella understood that it was okay not to be good at everything. Everyone had their own strengths and weaknesses, and that was perfectly okay.

Sure, she might not be able to beat the magical creatures, but she was determined enough to try. She also had some fantastic friends and great parents. She was clever in many classes at school, but she was bad at chess. Her other friend was better than her at swimming, and that was okay.

Ella smiled to herself, and with that newfound wisdom, she returned to the school with a newfound appreciation for her own strengths, weaknesses, and her friends.

When she returned to school, she made a special effort to be kinder to her friends and appreciate their strengths, no matter how different they were from her own. That day, she learned a valuable lesson: Everyone is good at something, but not everything. And that was okay!

And thanks to that day, Ella never felt superior or jealous of anyone ever again. Instead, she embraced the differences between all magical creatures and humans, celebrating their individual strengths and weaknesses with kindness and respect.

And that is why, to this day, Ella continues to be a champion of kindness whenever she can.

The Girl Who Thought She Knew Everything

Priya was not a curious girl. In fact, she thought she knew everything anyway, so what was the point in asking questions?

When she went to school, she never asked the teacher what they meant because she already knew the answer. How could she not? She was already the smartest girl in school.

Priya never asked how her friends were because she could already tell. There was no mystery, big or small, that Priya didn't already know about or have an opinion of.

On her first day of the new school year, Priya refused to go.

"Why do I need to go for?" she asked. "I already know everything."

"Well, that can't possibly be true. You're only eight years old and haven't even been to another country."

"I don't need to go to another country. I can just look up what it's like online and know all about it. Just like I know everything that's going to happen at school today," she said.

"And what is going to happen at school today?" asked Mom.

"Well, I'm going to go into class, go to assembly, have the register taken, go to lessons, have lunch, have more lessons, and come home. And I already know what the teachers are going to say."

"So, you really think you know everything?"

"I do. I know I do."

Priya's dad and mom looked at each other and sighed.

"It's a shame, though, Priya. There are so many beautiful things out there to learn about. But if you're not open to learning them, you'll never know.

Me and your Mom are 50 years old. That's fifty times around the sun we've been, and we still don't know everything."

"That's because you're you and not me."

"Well, how about you go to school, and if everything is how you think it's going to be, we can talk about it later."

"And make sure you listen to people," said dad, "you never know what you could learn."

"Fine," said Priya with a shrug, and off to school she went. She didn't need to prove anything to her parents, so she wasn't going to. She was only going to school because she had nothing else booked in for the day.

She got onto the bus and sat next to her friend Lottie.

"Hello, Lottie," Priya said.

"Hey, Priya. How are you?"

"Good. My parents are really something today, and it's not fair."

"Oh, how come?"

"They keep saying that I should listen to people and that I don't know everything."

"And do you really think you know everything?"

"I do. Of course. How could I not?"

"Okay then, what's in those woods?" Lottie pointed out the bus window at a forest they were passing by.

"Well, trees and grass, obviously. Other plants and insects too. Maybe a deer."

"Oh, that's so obvious, Priya. What else is in there? What else is in there that makes that forest extra special?"

"Nothing. It's just a forest."

"Okay," said Lottie. "Let's go and find out then?"

"Sure. And I'll prove to you, just like my parents, that I know what's going on."

"Let's do it."

Lottie and Priya got off the bus and spent the whole day at school. As Priya predicted, everything was as she said it would be. However, there was one difference. At the end of the school day, they didn't get back on the bus. Instead, they walked through the town and into the woods Lottie had pointed out.

They held each other's hands and walked deeper into the trees.

Just as Priya had predicted, everything looked just how she had imagined. There were trees and grass and small plants everywhere. There was even a little stream in one place, just as Priya could have imagined if she had thought about it hard enough.

However, an hour went by, and the girls were very much in the thick of the forest.

"Erm, Priya," said Lottie. "I think we may be lost. Do you know where we're going?"

Of course, Priya knows everything.

"Absolutely. We just need to go straight down this way, and we'll be back on the road. No problem."

"Are you sure? How could you possibly know that?"

"I just do, okay?"

"Okay then."

And so, the girls continued to walk into the forest. However, the more they walked, the darker the forest got, and even Priya started to get a little worried, but she remained headstrong. She knew what she was doing.

After another hour, the girls were still lost in the now dark and eerie forest. Both girls stayed quiet, listening to the weird groans and shouts the animals and trees were making. Although neither of them admitted it, they were both scared.

Things got even scarier.

"Oh, I think we've been here before," said Lottie. "This tree looks so familiar. Are we just going around in circles?"

"No, we're heading in the right direction," said Priya, although she was starting to think she didn't know at this point.

Just as Priya was speaking, there was the CRACK of a stick behind them. The girls spun around to see an old woman, hunched over, dressed in a black robe with a big pointy hat. She held something in her hand and cackled quietly in the silence.

The two girls froze and held each other closely. This was surely a witch. Hopefully, not a wicked old witch, Lottie thought to herself.

"Well, well, well, what do we have here?" the witch cackled to herself. She started to rub her hands together.

"Looks like lunch to me!"

The girls held each other tighter, both unsure of what to do.

"Now," the witch continued. "According to the law of the forest, I can't just take you away and eat you up for lunch. I have to give you a way out. I know, I know. It's not fair, but that's the rules, and I must stick to them."

"So," she continued. "The rules are quite simple. I ask you three questions, and you answer them. Get all three right, and I'll show you the way out. Get one wrong, and you will spend the rest of your life in my cauldron. Sounds fair?"

The witch burst into laughter that echoed around the entire forest, causing birds to fly up into the air in fear.

"Priya, I'm really scared."

"Me too," said Priya. "Me too."

"You'll know the answers to these questions, right?" Lottie asked.

Priya gulped. "I really hope so."

"Hey, you girls," the witch shouted. "No more talking. It's time to answer the first question. Here we go!"

"So, the first question, let's start with an easy math question to get us warmed up. What is ten times ten?"

The girls looked at each other as Priya was filled with confidence. This is going to be easy. How could she ever doubt herself? She knew everything, right?

"Easy," Priya said, stepping forward confidently, "it's 100."

"Oh, very good, my child, very good. Nice to know you have a big juicy brain inside your head. I bet this is going to taste delicious."

Priya ignored the witch and couldn't help but have a smug look on her face.

"Okay, second question, which countries do elephants come from?"

Priya thought for a moment. Countries? Well, obviously, elephants come from Africa. Everyone knows that. But another country? She thought about it some more. She knew there were two types of elephants. African and Indian elephants. Indian elephants were known for their bigger ears and bigger tusks! Therefore, the answer was simple.

"Africa and India! Easy."

"Ah," the witch laughed louder than she had before. "Excellent! That's just beautiful and so good, you clever little cookie. Looks like I'm going to be showing you out of the forest after all! Time for the last question. Are you ready?"

Priya looked at Lottie. They both smiled at each other. They had this.

"Third and final question. What is yours but is mostly used by others?"

Priya stopped in her tracks. Yours but used by others? Your bank card? Phone? A toy? No, none of those things. Priya started to panic and not think straight.

Umbrella? School pens? Books? No, no, no. Priya couldn't think. She turned back to Lottie, who was now standing beside her.

"I don't know the answer," she whispered. "I think we're going to be eaten. It's all my fault."

Priya started to cry, her cries echoing around the forest.

"Yes, cry away, little girl. If you can't get the answer, then you're both going to be my dinner!"

"Don't be silly," whispered Lottie into Priya's ear. "You don't need to be sad because you don't know everything. We're friends and can help each other out. Here, let me do this one."

Lottie stepped forward to face the wicked witch.

"Your name. Your name is something that's yours that other people use."

"AH!" said the witch, "how did you both get to be so clever? Ah, now I'll never have a tasty dinner, and I'll have to eat insects and bugs as I have done for years!"

The girls smiled at each other.

"Fine," said the witch, "fine. I'll show you to the exit."

And so the girls followed the witch through to the edge of the woods and back where they came in, allowing them to find their way home before dinner time.

Before the girls went into their own houses, Priya pulled Lottie aside.

"I'm really sorry about today. And always."

"Sorry for what?"

"Well, if I didn't pretend that I knew everything, we wouldn't have gone into the woods. We wouldn't have gotten lost, and if I was on my own or you weren't so clever, a wicked witch might have eaten us."

"It's quite alright, Priya," said Lottie, "as long as we're safe and sound now!"

They hugged each other and said goodbye.

Priya learned a valuable lesson that day - listening to others can be just as important as knowing it all. Just because she thought she knew everything didn't mean that she was always right. Priya now listens to what others have to say and understands the importance of asking questions.

The Fashion Show Disaster

When Eva was younger, she wanted to be the star of a fashion show. She dreamed of being so beautiful and having all eyes on her. It was all she ever wanted and more!!

She was obsessed with her looks, tried all the latest trends, and would do whatever it took to make herself look even better. Every day, she would wake up and spend hours in front of the mirror, trying to make herself look exactly like the girls in the magazines.

Of course, it was only natural that as Eva grew up, she decided she wanted to test how beautiful she was in the local talent show. And so she did. She was determined to win, no matter what it took. Though she had some nice clothes of her own, they weren't enough for her—she wanted to look the best.

"Hmm," Eva thought to herself, "where am I going to get the most beautiful clothes that will help me win the fashion show?"

First, she decided to ask her parents.

"Hey mom. Hey dad," she said, at breakfast one morning. "How are my favorite parents?"

"Good, thank you Eva. You're being extra happy and kind today. What's going on?"

"Oh nothing," said Eva. "I'm just feeling very happy and love you guys so much. I just wanted to let you know."

"Aww, well that's very nice, sweetie. We love you so much too."

"I was wondering though, you know I've been really good this year and my birthday is only around the corner? I was wondering if I could have my presents early, and ask for some lovely clothes for my competition."

Her parents looked at each other.

"Now Eva, you can't just say things like that. You can't just tell someone you love them because you want something from them."

Eva started to get angry. Of course she loved them, and all she was doing was asking for something to help her live her dreams. Isn't that what parents were for anyway?

"I didn't! I'm just saying that I want to win and I want to get some clothes to help me win. I thought you would support me in something that I wanted to do!"

"Of course we support you, but you already have so many nice, expensive clothes and outfits, and there's no reason you can't wear some of them."

"Urgh. You guys just never even try to understand me or help me."

"Well, that's just not true. All we do is think about you and do things to help you. Where do you think all the food in the house, and the house itself came from?"

Eva didn't want to hear it.

"Look Eva," her mom said. "We'll think about it, okay? But you can't get what you want by manipulating people. That's mean. It's unfair, and you wouldn't like it if people did that to you."

Eva wasn't listening. She was packing her school bag and out the door, thinking of new ways to get the best outfit for the upcoming competition. If her parents weren't going to help her make her dream come true, then she would have to figure it out on her own.

So, Eva went to school, playing with ideas in her head about how she was going to get the perfect outfit.

At school, she walked through the playground and couldn't help but notice her friends' beautiful outfits. Some of her friends had the most beautiful scarves. Others had the jackets she had always wanted. And Mary's shoes! They were exactly what she needed.

Urgh, Eva thought to herself. If mom and dad won't help me, and I don't have any money, I'm never going to get the winning outfit.

Classes started and Eva and her classmates started to go through the school day. However, when it came to the lesson before lunch, P.E, she had an idea.

If everyone is getting changed and leaving their clothes in the changing room, perhaps this would be a good time to borrow them. "I could only borrow them until the end of the week and then give them back next week after the fashion show is over," Eva thought. "Yes, that would work!"

And these clothes were from her friends. Eva was sure they wouldn't mind.

So, PE came around and all the girls got changed and ran out onto the football field. Eva went with them too, but just as she got onto the field, she started to cough.

"Oh no," said Miss Johnson, the sports teacher, "is everything okay Eva?"

"I don't think so, Miss. I'm feeling really sick."

"Yeah, that cough doesn't sound too good. Run back to the changing rooms and go to the nurse's office so they can look you over."

Eva nodded and walked back to the changing room. Now was her chance.

In an instant, she walked around the changing room, taking everything she needed from the hooks and shelves. Jacket. Scarf. Shoes. Cleo's beautiful top. And a hat. Perfect. Eva had everything she needed.

Stuffing the clothes into her bag, she ran off to the nurse's office, pretended to be sick, and got sent home.

She spent the next few days at home in bed, reading books, and practicing her catwalk, before saying she felt better on Friday night and was well enough to do the competition.

"Are you sure you want to go honey?" said her mom. "You don't have to if you're feeling unwell."

"No, it's all good. I feel much better now."

"Are you sure? We didn't get any new clothes either because we thought you'd be too sick."

"No, that's okay mom. I love you and it's fine. I'll go with what I have."

She gave her mom a kiss and had an early night, making sure she got enough beauty sleep for the show tomorrow.

The next day, Eva got dressed in some casual clothes, heading off to the competition with her new, borrowed outfits in her bag.

The competition was so busy and lots of girls ran backwards and forwards, some with their parents, some with their friends, getting ready for the big show. Eva had come on her own. She wanted her parents and friends to come and see her to support and cheer her on, but she couldn't invite them because they'd see she borrowed their clothes. She would have asked them, but with a competition this big, she couldn't risk them saying no.

And so, Eva got ready in her area of the changing room, putting on her new outfit and make up, and was ready to rock and roll.

Of course, with such amazing makeup and the best outfit around, Eva won the competition hands down! When the announcer called her name, she raised both hands in the air and cheered! The rest of the girls clapped and left the stage, and Eva was given a big trophy.

Then she was asked to give a little speech.

"Thank you for this award. Winning this competition is all I've ever wanted and I'm so happy to be here. I want to say a big thank you to…"

And Eva stopped talking.

She looked around at the crowd and the rest of the contestants. Everyone was with their friends and family. One of the girls who had lost was crying and had her friends and parents wiping away her tears. Some girls were looking at her, happy that she was able to win, their parents standing behind them proud.

Eva, on the other hand, was alone.

Eva couldn't finish the rest of her speech. She ran off the stage in tears and to her section in the dressing room. She had been so stupid. Yes, she wanted to win the competition, but at what cost?

She had lied and been mean to her parents. She had stolen and lied to her friends and parents. And now she was here alone with nobody she loved around her. Oh, how she hoped that her friends and family still loved her.

Her obsession drove everyone around her away. Eva went back home and called up all her friends, but they had all seen Eva on TV wearing their clothes, and didn't want to speak with her.

She had become so consumed by the idea of beauty that she was willing to do anything to get it, including taking from others and not caring about how it made them feel.

At that moment, Eva realized how wrong she had been. She shouldn't have taken from her friends and she shouldn't have been so obsessed with beauty. It was what she said and did—not how she looked—that truly made her a beautiful person.

That night, Eva felt better than ever before: she knew that it was important to be kind and that beauty came from within. It took a while to make things better. She gave all her clothes back to her friends and said sorry to everyone, and eventually her friends forgave her, and she had certainly learned the valuable lesson to be nice and caring to the people she loved, to be honest and caring towards them, and to give them real love forever more.

Bullies Be Gone

It was the end of another long and difficult day at school. It had been a difficult term. Riley was tired and it was as though life just didn't want her to be happy. She didn't get really high grades. They weren't the lowest, but they weren't what she wanted them to be. She dressed okay, and had some really nice friends. She felt like she lived a pretty typical life where not a lot of crazy things happened, and she certainly didn't do anything to make other people feel sad or hurt.

However, for some reason, the girls in her class had decided that they were going to bully her at every chance. Whether in class, before or after school, or during lunch break, these girls seemed to find Riley wherever she was and make her life horrible.

They would steal and hide her stuff. They would draw rude pictures in her textbooks. They would even tell the teachers horrible things Riley hadn't actually done and ended up getting her in a lot of trouble.

Riley told herself repeatedly that nothing was wrong with her, but it didn't seem to make a difference. The bullies had decided they would pick on her, and that was that.

"Was there really anything wrong?" she asked herself as she cried in bed. "Why was she crying?"

Riley was sure she hadn't done anything wrong to deserve the other girls' treatment. She didn't think she deserved such unkindness and disrespect, but what could she do?

She thought long and hard about how to stand up for herself and deal with the bullies creatively. She knew she couldn't fight them, and she didn't want to stoop to their level either.

She thought about it for a few days before speaking with her older sister, Maria, about it.

"What's up, sis," Maria said as Riley went to her room and knocked on the door.

"I was just wondering if I could speak to you, Maria."

"Sure, what's up? Come sit on the bed."

Riley sat on the edge of Maria's bed and told her everything that had happened. She said she'd done nothing wrong to these girls or hurt them. She hadn't even spoken to them before the beginning of term, and now suddenly, they were picking on her every chance they got.

Maria sat and thought about it.

"Have you told anyone about this?" asked Maria.

"Kinda. I've told you, and my friends know about it. The bullies just seem to find me when I'm on my own."

"Well," said Maria. "I went through something very similar when I was your age, and it's really easy to deal with them when you know how."

Riley listened carefully, making sure she heard how to solve this problem.

"It might sound silly, but all you have to do is ignore them. Ignore the bullies, and they end up going away."

This was not what Riley wanted to hear.

"Ignore them? How is that going to work? They'll just be even meaner. And I can't just ignore people who are calling me names and taking my stuff. What did I ever do to upset them?"

"Well, that's just it," said Maria, "you haven't. But they say things to make you feel bad, and you start questioning what you did wrong. You think you are all the bad things they say, and that's how they can keep doing what they do. It sounds weird, I know, but do you know what I mean?"

"Not really," said Riley.

"Well, you've been thinking about what you've done wrong and what's wrong with you."

"Yes. A little."

"The truth is, you haven't done anything wrong. But when you doubt yourself, and you're not sure of yourself, then you can't stand up for yourself or ignore what they're doing because you're always thinking to yourself, well, what if they're right and I have done something wrong?"

"So, if I'm sure of myself, I can ignore them, and they won't bother me anymore?"

"That's it! And stay with your friends, of course. If they're picking on you when you're alone and not with your friends, then stay with them."

"And if I'm not with my friends?"

"Try to be, but if you're not, then that's when you get the chance to ignore them!"

"But how can I be more sure of myself?"

"Let's do it now, shall we?" said Maria.

Maria took two pens and two sheets of paper out of her drawer and gave one to Riley.

"Now," said Maria, "I want you to write down all the amazing things about yourself. It can be anything. Even if you're only a little bit good at something, write it down. Like me, I'm not very creative, but I am a little bit, so I'll write it down!"

The two sisters spent a few minutes writing down all the things they loved about themselves. Riley wrote about how creative she was, how she did well in school and had lots of lovely friends. She wrote about how she was fast at running and drawing and made delicious cakes with her mom at Christmas. She wrote loads of things down, no matter how small those things were. She even wrote down that she was good at writing lists of things that she was good at.

After a few minutes, Riley and her sister had nearly filled a whole page with the things that they were good at.

"See," said Maria. "There are so many things you're good at, and no way those bullies are right about you being a bad person. Now take this list, let it fill you with confidence, and ignore those bullies because they clearly don't know what they're talking about."

Riley nodded, hugged her sister, and thanked her. It was amazing to see how many amazing and good things she actually did have going for her, and there was no way the bullies could be right.

The next day when Riley saw the bullies in school, instead of getting angry at them, she smiled and reminded herself of all the things she was proud of. She could ignore their comments and focus on her own self-worth, which gave her the strength to stand up for herself and speak out when she needed to.

This is My Chair

Once upon a time, there was a little girl named Jackie.

She was a kind and curious girl, and she loved nothing more than exploring her parent's fabulous garden. Her father was an amazing gardener; he had grown many beautiful trees and flowers over the years. There was everything, from roses to daffodils and even a pond full of fish and frogs. It was the most beautiful garden in the whole town, and everyone was welcome to come and enjoy it whenever they wanted! Her dad made sure of it.

One day, while exploring the garden on an adventure in the summer fun, Jackie stumbled across an old chair.

"Good," she thought to herself, "this is the perfect spot to rest from all my adventuring." She looked it over.

It was placed perfectly on the flat grass, with half of the chair in the bright sun and the other half in the gloriously refreshing shade. Sitting on the chair, she had a wonderful view of the pond and all the greenery and flowers around her.

Jackie smiled as she had found what felt like her very own special place in the garden. She claimed it as her own and said, "This is my chair." She would spend part of her afternoons here, enjoying the sun and reading her favorite book. It was all for her since she had discovered it and now claimed it.

But much to Jackie's frustration, all the bees and butterflies in the garden had other ideas.

First, it was the bees.

"Hey there, Jackie. How are you?" a bee buzzed as it flew around her chair.

"I'm amazing, thank you! It's such a beautiful day, and this is such a beautiful spot to admire the garden!"

"Wow, it really is! Do you mind if I sit here and enjoy it too?"

"Absolutely not," Jackie said in a stern voice. "This is my chair, and I got here first."

"Oh, but there's more than enough room for two," the bee said as he flew away, feeling sad.

Next, it was the butterflies. They all came fluttering around, bright and colorful and full of joy.

"Hey Jackie," they said. "This is such a beautiful chair you've found! Can we join you?"

Again, Jackie said with a stern voice, "No! This is my chair, and you're not welcome. I found it first, and I don't want you to take it from me."

"But, we wouldn't..."

"LEAVE!"

The butterflies flew away, feeling sad that Jackie wouldn't let them sit with her.

Next, two of Jackie's friends, Elsa and Joey, came by.

"Hey Jackie," they waved! "We saw you sitting in this chair and wanted to join you! The sun is so nice today, and it would be a lot of fun if we could all hang out together."

But Jackie said no. She didn't want to share her chair because she was feeling selfish. So, Elsa and Joey had to go away, feeling sad that Jackie wouldn't let them join her.

Soon enough, Jackie was alone again in her chair.

Finally, a cat came and landed on the chair next to Jackie. It stretched out its legs and started to clean itself.

"Hey, cat, what are you doing here?"

"I'm sorry, are you talking to me?" asked the cat, looking quite shocked that it had just been shouted at.

"Yes, I'm talking to you," said Jackie. "What are you doing on my chair?"

"Oh, this is your chair? Sorry, I didn't realize. I thought this was a chair that everyone in the garden could come and visit!"

"Absolutely not," said Jackie. "This is my chair; nobody else is allowed to sit here. I've been adventuring for a long time today, and this chair is all for me!"

"Oh, I see," said the cat. "Perhaps I can stay here a little..."

"GO!" shouted Jackie at the top of her voice. She yelled so loud that the cat jumped out of fright. Without saying another word, the cat took off to find somewhere else to sit.

Jackie took a deep breath to calm herself down and returned to enjoying her time on the bench. However, her peaceful time didn't seem to last long. After a few minutes, Jackie kind of missed the butterfly. And the bee. And her friends Joey and Elsa. And the cat. She soon decided it would be pretty nice and not so lonely if she had a friend to enjoy this beautiful part of the garden.

She took off to say sorry and to see if she could find anyone who still wanted to share the chair with her. She looked high and low throughout the garden but, much to her surprise, she couldn't find anyone to speak to. There were no bees, butterflies, cats, or friends to be found anywhere in the garden.

However, just as she was starting to give up hope, she heard laughter coming from the other side of a big hedge.

It sounded so joyful and happy that it made her smile. She decided to investigate, and to her surprise, there were all the bees, butterflies, and her friends. Even the cat played under the table, trying to catch its tail.

They had found their own chairs in the garden and were having a little garden party of their own!

"Hey, everyone," Jackie said sheepishly. "How are you?"

Everyone at the table stopped and turned around. They looked at her, and the cat stopped playing and sat up properly to look her way.

"Oh, hello," said the butterflies together. "What are you doing here?"

"I was just wondering if I could join your party? It looks like a lot of fun."

"No, absolutely not!" said the bees together.

"But if I could just..."

"I think you should just go," said the cat. Jackie looked at Joey and Elsa, sitting next to each other to cut a piece of cake. They turned away without saying a word.

Saddened and with a heavy heart, Jackie turned and went away from the party and back towards the house. It wasn't until she got into the house and closed the back door that she burst into tears. Her mother instantly came in from another room to see what was going on.

"Oh Jackie, is everything okay? Why are you crying?" she asked, giving Jackie a big hug and a kiss on top of her head.

Jackie told her all about the garden chairs and how she wouldn't let her friends join her.

"Oh, Jackie," her mother said with a hug, "sharing is much more fun, and it helps make everyone happy. Don't you think?"

"But I didn't want to share."

"And that's fine. You're allowed to do things by yourself, and if you don't want people to sit with you, that's fine. But then other people have that right as well. If they don't want to invite you to their party, then they don't have to. Just like you don't have to let them sit on your chair."

"But I felt really sad when they didn't invite me."

"Just like your friends felt sad when you said they couldn't share the garden chair with you."

Jackie thought about it. It made sense, and Jackie felt sad that she had made her friends feel as sad as she did.

Jackie's mom gave her a hug.

"When we share things," Jackie's mom said, "then everyone gets to enjoy all the fun things we're doing, and we won't feel so lonely when we get to do all these fun things with the people we love more than anything in the world."

Jackie agreed. Sharing is far more fun and far less lonely. She made her way to the garden party, and everyone went quiet when she walked over.

"Hey, everyone," she said, looking at the ground. "I'm sorry for being selfish with the garden chair. I could have shared it."

Her friends smiled and looked up.

"It's okay, Jackie. And of course, you're invited to the party! Let's have some fun!"

And so, Jackie and her friends started playing together and having lots of fun where they ate cake, danced to music, and had some beautiful fun in the summer sun! And, of course, Jackie learned the lesson that although she can choose to sit by herself from time to time and not share what she's got, she doesn't have to be rude about it, and it's usually going to be a lot more fun to share!

I Want Your Birthday

Today was Billie's mom's birthday.

The family was so excited because birthdays are always such a beautiful time of the year. As always, the day started with Billie and her sister Maeve running into mom's room to jump on the bed and snuggle their mom and dad.

After some gorgeous cuddles beneath the sheets and some rolling around, Maeve gave mom the biggest cuddle yet.

"Ah, girls, thank you so much for a beautiful wake-up. What a great way to start my birthday!"

Both girls smiled and nuzzled a little more.

"Oh, Maeve, your hugs are getting so big! You're growing so fast. I love you so much, Maeve," said mom, stroking Maeve's hair.

Billie looked at her younger sister getting a bigger hug from their mom, and a strange feeling came up in her chest.

"Hey," said Billie. "I want cuddles too! And I'm also growing!"

Mom smiled and opened her arms.

"Of course, Billie. Come here too!" They cuddled, and it was the best family hug ever. They stayed like this for a while and even watched an episode of cartoons in bed!

"Come on then, kids," said dad, "it's time for us to make mom her special birthday breakfast."

And so dad, Billie, and Maeve went to the kitchen, everyone helping in different ways. Billie and Maeve's job was adding some strawberries to the pancakes that dad made.

"Mmm," said Billie. "I like pancakes. I want some pancakes for myself," chirped Billie, her eyes twinkling with excitement.

"No, no," said Maeve and Dad in unison, "these are for mom's birthday breakfast. It's a special surprise!"

Billie sighed, "I know, but they look so good!" and added strawberries.

"We'll give these pancakes to mom so she can enjoy her morning in bed, and we'll come back and make some more for us afterward. How does that sound?"

"Fine," said Billie, and shrugged her shoulders before going back to strawberry duty.

After breakfast was made and eaten in bed, it was time for gifts.

Mom had so many presents stacked up on the bed. She started to unwrap them, one after the other. She had received a beautiful necklace from her best friend, a new set of cooking utensils from dad, and some delicious chocolates from the kids.

Billie wanted a gift so badly she could almost taste it! Her birthday was four months ago, and she wouldn't receive any more presents until Christmas. She wanted to open just one present so badly!

"I want the presents," said Billie, her eyes still twinkling with excitement.

Mom laughed, "No, sweetheart, these presents are for me! You'll get your presents soon."

Billie was disappointed.

"Please, mom. I want a present! WHY CAN'T I GET A PRESENT!"

"Hey now," said dad, "It's your mom's special day, so we should all be thinking about what she wants, not just what we want. We do the same for you on your special day."

"Urgh, fine," said Billie, and she sat quietly while the rest of the presents were being opened.

After brushing their teeth, tidying up wrapping paper, and clearing away breakfast, it was time to head out. Since it was mom's birthday, she had decided that they would go to the zoo for the day.

But Billie didn't want to go to the zoo. Billie wanted to go to the amusement park.

"I WANT TO PLAY!" said Billie, stomping her feet. "I WANT TO GO TO THE AMUSEMENT PARK!"

Mom and dad sighed and looked at each other.

"Billie," said Mom calmly, "today is my birthday, and I want to go to the zoo. We can go to the amusement park another day. We can go on your birthday, but I'm laying down my boundary because today, we focus on me. On your birthday, we focus on you."

Billie pouted and crossed her arms.

"No, no," said dad, "you need to understand that it's not always about you. Sometimes, we need to think about other people and what they want. That's how everyone can be happy."

"I don't want you to keep talking; you're making me sad!" said Billie with tears in her eyes.

"Okay, well, go and take some time in your room..."

"URGH" Billie stormed into her room and slammed the door behind her. She didn't want to go to her room. She wanted to have just one nice thing today.

Why did no one listen to her? Why did no one want to give her anything nice? She wasn't being selfish. Everyone else was being selfish and only thinking about mom! They always told her to share things with everyone else, especially Maeve, but apparently, nobody had to share with her in return!

It just wasn't fair.

A few minutes later, dad knocked on the door and opened it slowly.

"Hey, kiddo," he said softly, "we're sorry for shouting at you. We understand that you just want to have a nice day too. That's why it's important to think about other people and their wants. That way, we can all have a good time together. It's not always all about what Billie wants, what mom wants, me, or Maeve."

Billie sniffled and nodded in understanding. Dad smiled and hugged her. It was finally time for the zoo!

The rest of the day was spent exploring the zoo and having a blast. Billie had a lovely time with her family, and it was so much nicer to be there for her mom and family and do what everyone else was doing and not just what she wanted to do.

At lunchtime, the family went to the Jungle Cafe next to the giraffe for birthday lunch. Billie ordered fries and a cheeseburger, as a kid's meal of course, and everyone sat down to eat. Dad even got mom a little cupcake as a birthday treat.

After they ate, dad said that Billie and Maeve could go and play on the playground for a bit while the adults had a chat. Billie and Maeve loved playing at the playground, so they ran off and headed toward the biggest slide.

They climbed all the way to the top of the climbing frame and stood at the top of the slide. It looked so big and fast, and it was amazing that they could see all the nearby animals from up there. They were nearly up as high as the giraffes!

Then, just as Billie was about to get on the slide for the first time, she felt a large push come from the side. A big enough push to send her flying off to the side. There, right where she had been standing, was a tall girl who must have been a little bit older than her, lining up to take her turn.

"Hey," said Billie, "Why did you push in front of me?"

"Because it's not your turn," the girl said, and off she went down the side.

Billie waited until the girl was gone and lined up to have her turn again. But this time, more kids had come up to the top of the slide, and she had to wait for them to take their turn. Just when the line cleared, Billie lined herself up and felt that big PUSH again.

"Hey, I told you," the same older girl said, "It's not your turn. It's never your turn, and I want to have my go NOW."

Billie felt like crying. Maeve stood next to her and didn't say a word.

Billie let the older girl go down the slide and sat with Maeve feeling sad that this girl was so mean. The older girl came up to the top of the slide and slid down again several times, each time shouting at Billie, and the other kids, that it wasn't their turn and that she wanted to go NOW.

A few minutes passed, and dad called Billie and Maeve down so they would see the rest of the zoo. Dad instantly saw the tears on Billie's face as she climbed down.

"What's up, kiddo? Did you fall over or something?"

"No, Dad," said Billie. "There was a girl up there on the slide that kept pushing me out the way over and over again. Me and Maeve didn't even get one time to slide down."

"Oh dear, and she actually pushed you? Are you okay?"

"Yeah, I'm okay, but she was so selfish and mean. Why couldn't she just share…"

The thought clicked in Billie's head. She had been just like that older girl this morning. When her mom had wanted to enjoy opening her presents, Billie had jumped in and said that she wished for something instead, just as selfishly as the girl on the slide had.

In an instant, she ran up to her mom and gave her the biggest hug she had given her in such a long time.

"I'm really sorry for being selfish, mom, I know that it's wrong, and I didn't mean to spoil your birthday."

"You haven't spoiled anything," said mom, "now, let's go and have a lovely rest of the day at the zoo. Who wants ice cream?"

Everyone cheered and ran to the ice cream stand to enjoy the rest of mom's birthday the way it should be appreciated.

Things That Make Me Happy

Abbie was having an awful day.

It started first thing in the morning when Abbie woke up. She woke up and rolled over, rolled over in bed, only to notice she had turned to face the BIGGEST spider she had ever seen!

Instantly, Abbie had tried to brush it away with the book on her bedside table, but accidentally flicked it onto the floor. It started to walk back towards her and its huge, furry, creepy legs were so icky and yucky!

So yucky that she had to start screaming for her mom to come and take it away. Mom wasn't very happy about it, and told Abbie off for screaming and waking everyone up when they were fast asleep, but at least the spider was put out the window.

However, her bad luck continued. After getting dressed and going downstairs, Abbie made herself some cereal and sat down to read one of her favorite magazines while she ate. This was her favorite magazine because she always got to enjoy the little toy that came stuck to the front of the book.

But today, with her bad luck, when Abbie tried to open the toy, this time a little blue and white unicorn, the bag would not open. She struggled and struggled, trying to pull the bag open from both sides. Even mom tried to tell her how to open it, but it still didn't budge.

Abbie got so frustrated that she pulled the bag as hard as she could while trying to open it, and while it worked, she had pulled it so hard that she ended up knocking her cereal bowl over.

The cereal flew in one direction, and milk covered the floor, and herself! Her school uniform was ruined, and mom sounded really angry as she ran around the kitchen with a paper towel, trying to clean everything up quickly.

"UGH!" Abbie shouted. "Why does this always happen to me?"

The bad luck kept going all day for Abbie.

On her way to school, there was a traffic jam as all the cars tried to get past a broken down car, but this meant Abbie was really late and had to go into her first class ten minutes after everyone else.

Nobody liked being late because the teacher always had to say "excuse young sir or miss, why are you late to my class?" to which you always had to reply "I'm sorry, it won't happen again" and all the kids would laugh.

This day was also really bad because not just one, but both her best friends were off sick with coughs (it was winter you see, and mom always said there was some illness going around this time of year), so Abbie felt really alone.

She was having such a bad day she didn't want to spend time with anyone else, but it would be nice if the other girls asked her to come and dance with them. She would even settle for the boys coming to ask her to play football with them. Anything would be nice. She just didn't want to feel like nobody wanted to talk with her.

She couldn't even get anything to eat. She had been so late getting to school that mom hadn't even given her lunch money, and she only had enough money in her purse to buy the cheapest, oldest cheese sandwich. It tasted so bad.

Abbie tried to make it better by breaking the sandwich into some fun little triangles, but each piece was so small that she couldn't pick it up, and they all fell apart. She gave up and threw the sandwich in the bin.

Instead, Abbie spent the rest of her break and lunch time walking around the playground, kicking stones into bushes and picking at bits of flaky paint from the walls.

Of course, she got told off by the Head of Year for doing this, and was told to go and sit on the field and wait for afternoon classes to begin.

"Urgh," Abbie thought to herself. "This day cannot get any worse."

But it did.

Afternoon classes started with French, which was her worst subject. Mr. Tech, the French teacher, seemed to hate Abbie because he always picked on her to answer the hardest questions.

"Quelle est la date d'aujourd'hui?" he would ask, which meant "What is today's date?"

"C'est mercredi aujourd'hui," Abbie answered, which meant "It's Wednesday today."

"And the number?" Asked Mr. Tech.

Abbie didn't know. She didn't even want to know. She just wanted to cry and go home and go to bed without milk on her school clothes and without the spider trying to join her.

Mom picked her up after school, but she was busy on the phone talking about work things. Abbie felt alone. She wanted someone to make her smile and to tell her everything was going to be okay. She wanted to tell her mom all the things that had happened during the day, but every time she tried, all her mom said was "Ssh Abbie, can't you see I'm busy talking on the phone?"

Before going home, they stopped off at the clothes store to pick out a dress for a family party that was happening at the weekend. The store was in town and, being winter, it was already way too dark and way too cold to be outside.

"But, mom," said Abbie. "I don't want to go to town. It's cold, and I don't want to walk around. Can we please just go home?"

"No, Abbie," she said. "We need to go and pick out some dresses today. Otherwise, what are you going to wear for the party? All the family members are going to be there, so we need to make sure we're looking our best."

"I don't want to!" Abbie moaned, but her mom took her by the hand and made her do it anyway.

Abbie was so grumpy. She looked around town, annoyed at all the people who seemed so happy. WHY CAN'T THIS DAY JUST END ALREADY, Abbie thought to herself.

Even the birds in the trees sounded like they were having more fun than her!

But then, as if by magic, something changed.

The birds in the trees were singing their songs, and it sounded absolutely beautiful. So beautiful, in fact, that it didn't even seem to be cold and dark outside anymore. It actually felt really lovely. She looked around and it was as if she was seeing the world for the first time.

Instead of just looking at the floor and watching the stones go by, feeling sad, and put down by how bad the day had been, she was seeing everything in color! The squirrels raced about up and down trees and across the paths, gathering and burying their nuts for the winter.

The swans on the river peacefully floated up and down, calling out to each other every now and then. When they reached the little cafe, there were a few people inside and outside, sipping their drinks, petting their dogs, and laughing. Down the road, an old man sat on a bench feeding breadcrumbs to a group of pigeons at his feet.

When Abbie looked up, even though it was still day time, there wasn't a cloud in the sky, and she could even see a full moon!

All these amazing and beautiful things were right in front of her, and Abbie thought it was crazy that she hadn't seen any of it before. It was as though someone had suddenly turned on a beautiful switch for the whole planet!

Abbie and her mom finally reached the store, and Abbie fell in love with all the bright and beautiful dresses. She spent the next hour going around touching all the dresses, trying a few of them on, feeling the materials, and simply just enjoying being in the room with her mom. Even her mom joined in and seemed much happier than she had been all day!

So, Abbie took a deep breath and smiled. She was grateful for the opportunity to pick out her own dress for the party. She was also grateful that she could just be happy if she chose to focus on the good things.

As she picked her dress out, she noticed how bright and beautiful it was, and she thanked her mom for taking her out. She was really grateful for her mom for always being there for her and doing all the beautiful things she always did. She really was the best mom in the whole entire world.

Abbie learned a valuable lesson that day: even on the worst of days, if you look for the good things and focus on how grateful you are, even the worst day can become much brighter.

Conclusion

Thank you for taking the time to read through this wonderful book, Inspiring Stories for Girls: Girl, You're Amazing - A Collection of Stories About Self-Confidence, Courage, and Determination. I hope you found some new favorites and have maybe had the opportunity to look at life in some new, interesting, and exciting ways.

That's all from me for now, but I would love to hear your thoughts on this book moving forward! Wherever you picked up your copy, simply leave a review letting me know what you loved or what you want to see next time.

And trust me, I'm reading them all, and I look forward to hearing from you!

Until next time, I'll see you soon, but don't forget to look after yourself! It's a big, wide world, and it's easy to get lost and scared with every twist and turn. But remember: You're an inspirational girl who's confident, courageous, and has so much love to bring into each and every day.

With all my love for you,

- Ruby